I've done nothing wrong today

Alex Ingram

Alex Ingram

All rights reserved, no part of this publication may be reproduced by any means, electronic, mechanical photocopying, documentary, film or in any other format without prior written permission of the publisher.

    Published by
    Chipmunkapublishing
    PO Box 6872
    Brentwood
    Essex CM13 1ZT
    United Kingdom

http://www.chipmunkapublishing.com

Copyright © Alex Ingram 2008

www.myspace.com/alex_ingram

Alex Ingram

The idea of writing a foreword of any kind has daunted me, the apprehension coming from attempts to write an artist's Statement at Art School. It seemed the work was always changing in subject matter as well as process and it seemed the exercise of producing a statement would prove restrictive by the very nature of having to describe my work.

As an artist I have worked in many mediums but for the aims of this book, which I hope you enjoy, I'd like to focus on my photography and video work to illustrate how my works are attempts at 'making a mess' and 'tidying up' the world around me and how I see primarily these processes as my tools in doing so.

I look at how these processes affect 'the continuum', a sequence of events on a timeline. In this respect I view the process of videoing as 'tidying up'. If a piece is three minutes long it records all three minutes, the whole continuum. By contrast photography leaves the continuum in a mess, the effect is of each photo taking pieces of the continuum away, leaving a sequence of events with gaps in them. This when viewed as a whole is not continuous, a mess.

With the work itself, my choices as to the nature of the material, I see myself basically making a mess in my videos, carrying out activities that allow me to make a change in my environment through physicality. A mess being seen as bringing movement to an environment that was still, static. My effect on objects and surroundings is mess making. With my videos, pursuing the moment is very important to me. Letting the possibility of a happening occur, with only the basics planned for, free action, loose results.

However, with the photographs although making a mess of the continuum, the act of collecting these images (pressing the button) is very much like tidying up. I tidy up my environment by focussing on specific parts of it. As well as this the grouping and editing of these images into meanings, juxtapositions have served as a valuable ordering tool, allowing me to be very specific in what I say.

The writing has been included as it is an integral part of my work. It is linked to both my videoing and photography, in that they all record my activities. I see videoing as capturing the activity, my photographs collecting traces of action, with the writing being about doing things (making lists, taking Mary on the road).

Maybe the hope is that through all this making a mess and tidying up, I'll have done nothing wrong today.

Alex Ingram

The Creative Being

The creative being fell like a landscape and moulded itself around the room, fitting over the table and chairs, tucking itself neatly under legs and pens. Its spell made every movement one of magic, and moments sparked off each other turning objects into opportunities and touch into a glorious instrument.

Asking nothing in return, except to be present, the boy accepted its gift and began to make art. He revelled in unforeseen relationships, the beauty of the everyday, and a new-found appreciation of his world.

However as time went on he began to become secretive and place value on his creations. Aware of the being's eyes, this consciousness began to stifle the boy and he began to see his processes thwarted by mistakes. Seeing him struggle, the being reassured that these were vital parts of his creations and it was no-one's fault. The boy didn't believe him, feeling there was no room for both of them in the activities he wished to pursue. He dismissed the creative being who graciously rose as he had fallen, leaving the debris he had blessed with his presence.

Truly alone the boy sometimes remembers the creative being with fondness, tempted to invite it back into his life.

Alex Ingram

Alex Ingram

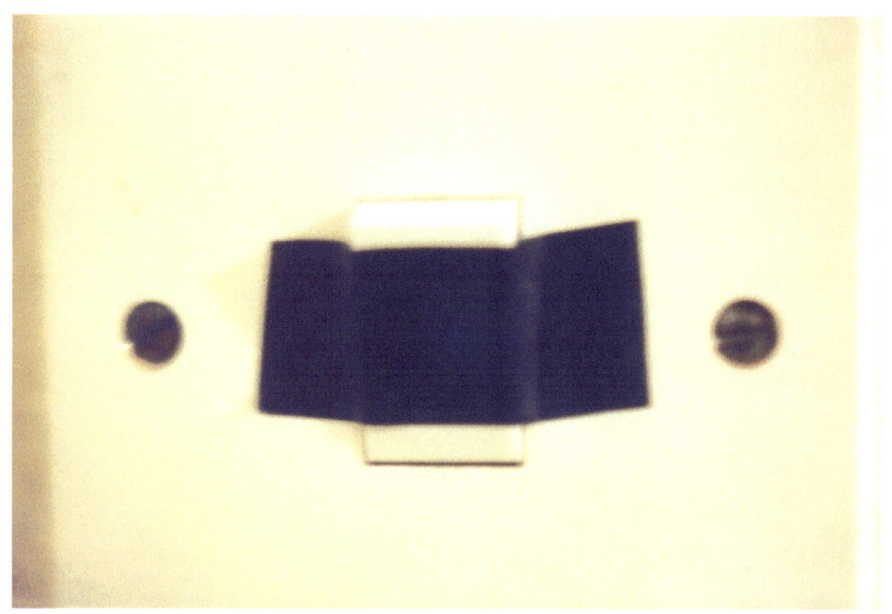

Alex Ingram

Alex Ingram

Blackout Bob suffered from worry, sections had been sliced out of his brain. His imagination revisited the vacant structures he had walked in, apprehensive of situations that may occur within them. Memories came from nothing and suddenly ended in blackness.

His self-diagnosis was that of blackouts, never discussing it with a doctor and not trusting friends or family, as a secret kept is calm as a lake, and his belief made him sane although he did worry.

Finding the walls of comfort, he stayed within his room, picking at the paper in apathetic attempts at making peepholes into an abundance of stories, where he wished to find a history to place himself in.

He didn't know how he could believe the tales he belonged to, that others told him of. He knew he needed a base and couldn't raise his hopes without falling to an unsteady floor.

For he didn't know himself, and his past was riddled with expanding spaces waiting to be filled in. No proof, everything seemed possible and without substance. Worry, worry, worry, worry. Bob decided to close his eyes every now and again, finding quietness a blessed relief.

Alex Ingram

Alex Ingram

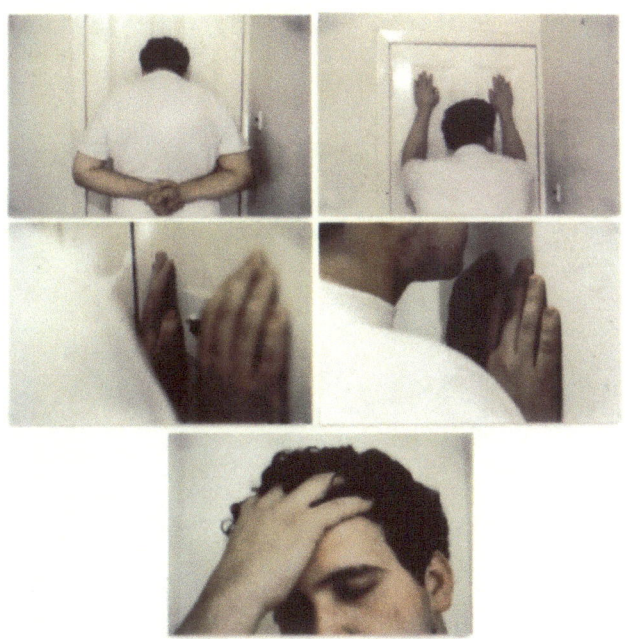

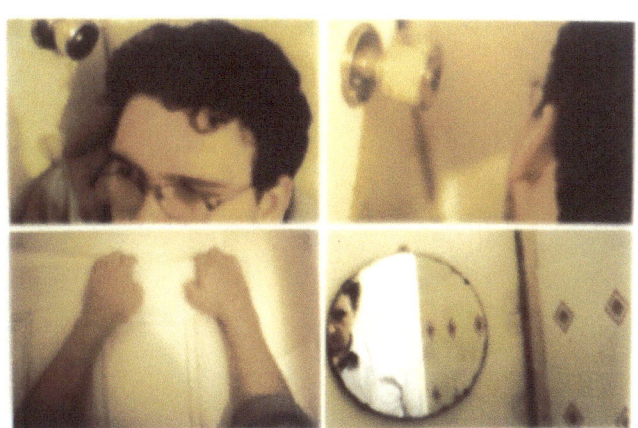

Alex Ingram

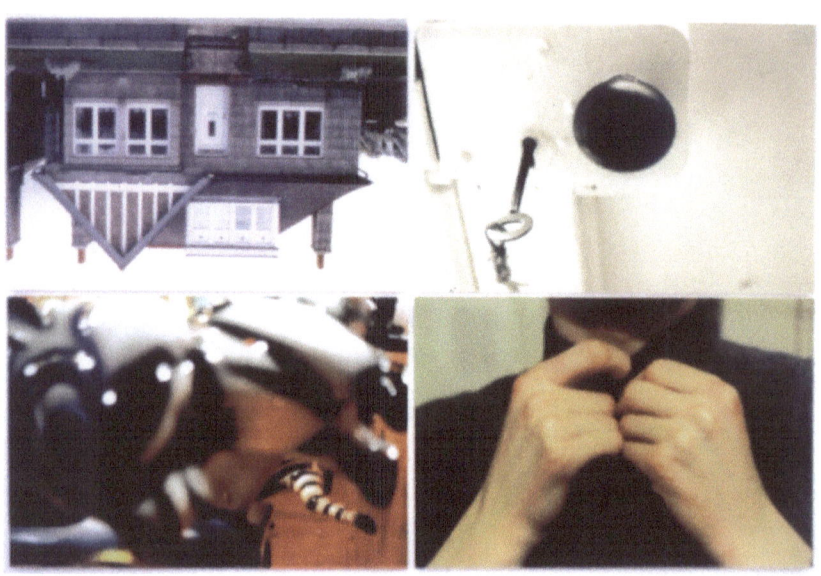

Alex Ingram

Alex Ingram

Alex Ingram

Alex Ingram

The boy who ran away with himself was tired of making lists. He knew as he grew older he'd pass them off as great works of art. Being quiet, shy and inconspicuous, he knew that the overheard conversations and colour combinations would eventually masquerade into stories with no story, narratives for the appetite of those listing themselves as well.

So he decided for life to catch him instead of him catching life. To let slip the information around him and let his thoughts wander. To see and hear what happened, to let go of the seductiveness of noticing everything. That things are what they are in the continuousness of a lifetime, and not everything is asking to be recorded.

For how much could he say or write, from making lists where the equality of each notion, phrase and gesture was undoubted, he wished to learn the importance of discernment. That if two was two, it didn't need to become four, and the sum would have no purpose in the bath or in front of the TV.

Alex Ingram

Alex Ingram

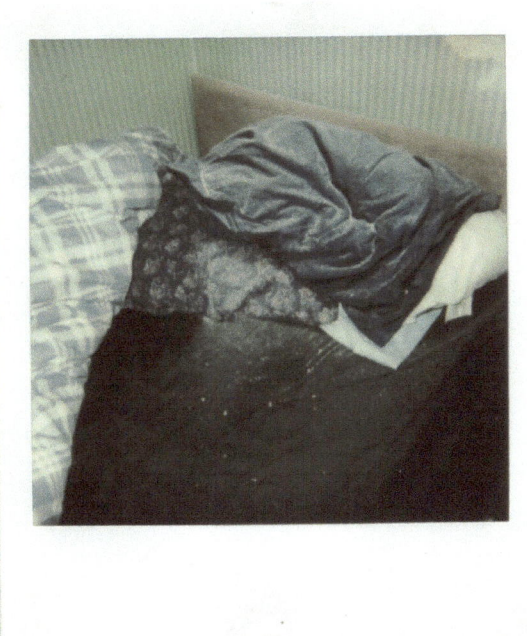

Alex Ingram

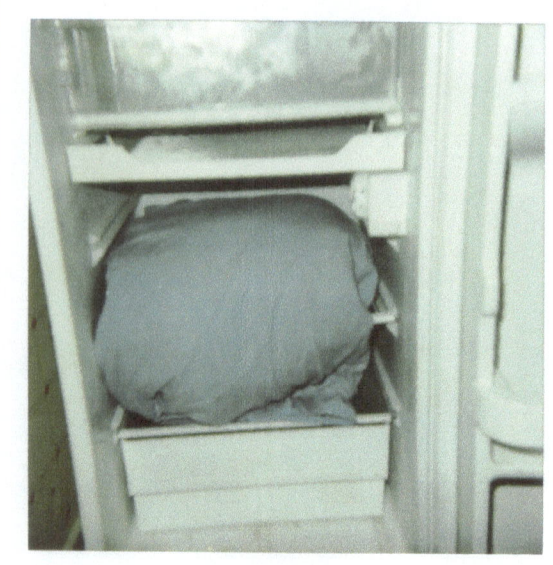

The Fool

The fool, who didn't know, could not face the world. His axis was spun by others with advice and opinions that left him disorientated and confused.

Swinging, he knew nothing and balanced between uncertainty and fear, he questioned the depth and duration of the next drop.

Standing in the middle of the sea he tied string around a stone and lowered it slowly to the bottom. Pinching at the wet length, he measured and tugged it up to the surface.

On a chilly and deserted day his retrieval was unsuccessful, his string came back empty. The fool was left with a question.

He tried to blame the fishes that he'd never seen: the crabs that must clutter the sea bed: or even a mischievous mermaid.

Where was the stone? He did not know, and was certain no one did either. The fool was no longer alone, he was one of the many. He realized that the advice and opinions of others were substantial to themselves and were like the invisible hands that populate the depths of the sea- too many to shake, and at best the maker of pretty waves to throw stones in.

Alex Ingram

Alex Ingram

Alex Ingram

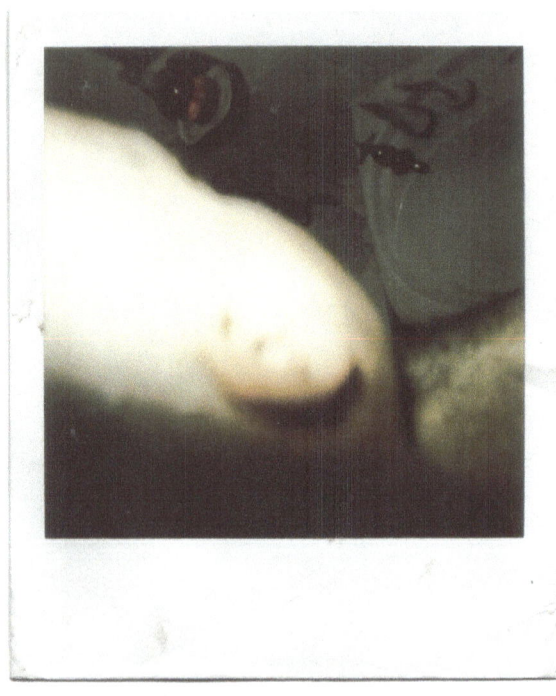

Alex Ingram

Alex Ingram

The writer of sad thoughts

The writer of sad things had plenty of material, or so he thought. A lapsed memory would plague him and, in recalling what had gone, many an unfinished sentence weighed on his page. Broken lines, the unfinished and hopeless state of thoughts.

Nudged out of the view, for a moment his eyes were filled with silence, its sweetness lost on a perplexing need to recall. The need to tell, a gift of woe was given to his nearest and dearest, the lines of their hands cupped and creased in support.

Not enough, the patience of each was abundant. Never truly alone and depressed in company, he didn't know why he had a consoling face to tell of his disheartednees with himself.

Under the ledge he couldn't understand how at one time he had been happy, the stones he was swallowing now had the gritty taste of truth.

He had known many mind men whose pill prowess was profound and a regime was endorsed. Still amputated lines led nowhere and threatened to dangle annoyingly as waste of no value. Closure is for the fortunate and the lucky. And those without fortune or luck? They collect what they can and drag themselves from situation to situation in a sluggish vehicle called the body.

I wish I could say what the writer of sad things is doing now. He's probably finding the door a little harder to open, his steps are more likely to be louder that the next man's, and I'm sure his voice is still killing him.

Alex Ingram

Alex Ingram

Alex Ingram

Alex Ingram

Alex Ingram

Sinking man

He is so full of tears,
Every time he breathes
He treds water.

Alex Ingram

Runner

He speaks fast,
So no-one will ask him,
What his words mean.

As if a pause could let
The arrows and bullets in,
And the world would only get bigger.

Spring Sprung.

Green washed fresh by grey.
Pavements silver reflections.
Falling sunlit transparancies
And disintergrating winter illusions,
Flooding the system
With melting amorphic hearts.

High seas, Red clouds.

Flying without wings,
Directed without eyes,
Birds of only teeth,
Grab, steal and plunder,
The eggs of thought.

Alex Ingram

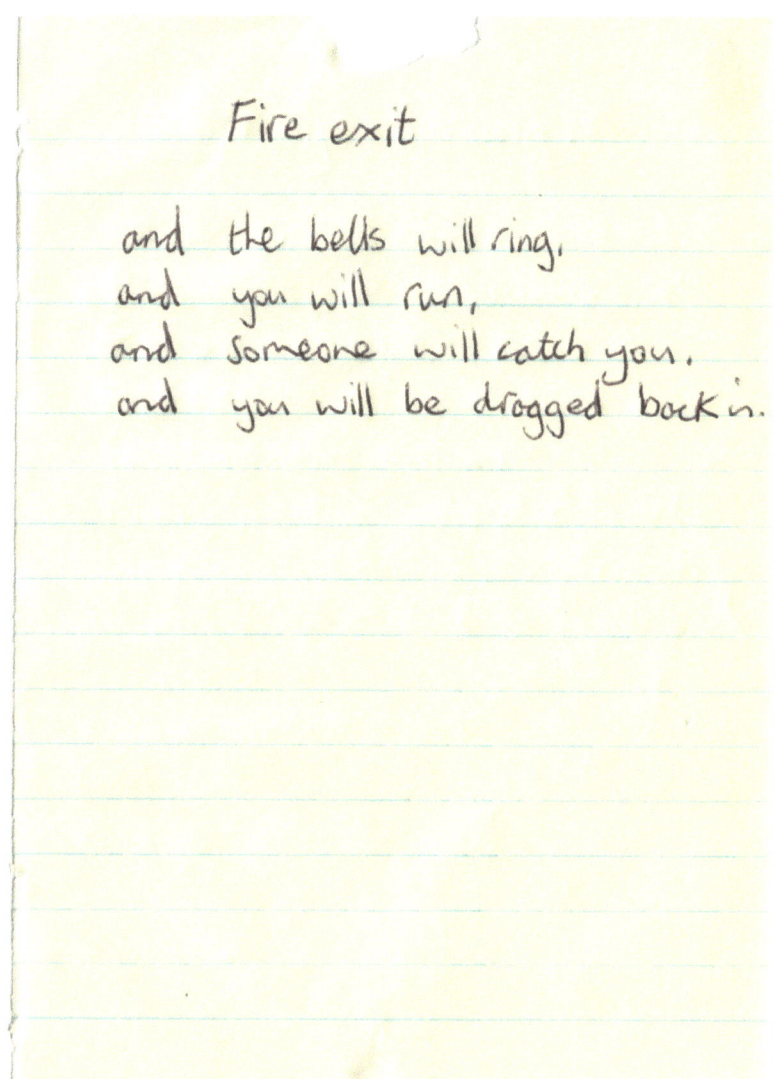

Fire exit

and the bells will ring,
and you will run,
and someone will catch you,
and you will be dragged back in.

Contentment

The quiet

A space where what was wrong has gone,

As if you could make ~~your~~
through it

Wading in the lake of your
living room.

Not happy or sad

But still.

Some people say I have eyes that could
Give you all the time in the world.

I say they're blue.
Other people say they're very blue.

I suppose that makes me lucky in
your eyes.

It makes me think you've got
nice eyes too.

The unexplained.

The aliens took him away,
When he was a baby,
And pressed his pleasure button.

They knew he would always know,
When he was happy.

And that a sunny day,
Would bring it out in him.

And now at twenty-six,
he constantly looks up at the sky.

The young man who cried clouds.

There was a young man whose eyes were so beautiful God could not bring himself to see them cry. Instead clouds would drift from his eyelids upwards into a welcoming breeze thankful to carry the bounty of God the young man posessed.

Clouds caught his head, rested under ears, neck, ~~hands~~ and legs lifting him upwards and pushing his hands away from his face.

As he rose from his chair his feet curled over pillows of air, knees curling above.

Floating, God sighed and brought the young man over forests and mountains, rivers and glades and so the young man travelled the world.

Alex Ingram

Resting Place.

Twenty thousand miles away,
Over land and under the sea
and under land again.
Is where he rests.
Cool and sweet like plankton mint
Growing in crystal blue gardens
without front or back door
to leave from,
beneath the swimming of folks
young and old,
open eyed and smiling.
bold as a shipwreck
And as graceful as a shoal.
Thats where he lies tonight,
with rested sails whose
gail catching days are over

"I sat still and imagined what else I knew to be out in the dripping yellow filter of the sun.
　Could upon an intimate crossing of fingertip on skin a melding of four eyes bring about one glance.
　And so my eyes dart like fish waiting to be caught and raised to an awaiting sky.
　　Sun
　　Sun
Take me, it has begun.

To find upon a found
like taking earth from a
mound
Is impressive as it sounds
Without parading it around
town.
　To loose what you've
found.
　Would be to brag
　without bounds

But to use neither luck
or logic.
Would be like releasing
the hounds.

So stand fast
and look with your
eyes and not your
hands.
And your search
may be your last.

In the woods

Fish dance and bear folly,
In the woods where we live
the animals play at eating each other,
and flowers sing in rich colour.

Yellow is never sickly
And green never looses to fatigue,
~~~~~ White is the gift of art,
cold and ready,
and black invites our eyes upwards.

Two men as two children,
heavy coated and light hearted
throwing into water and air,
without worry or care.

Taking Mary on the road

I came from a house called mary,
And when I left,
She followed like most houses of tender
Picking up her pansy boarders
and gravel skirt.
She addorned many a rooftop journey
from place to city
and places and cities.
to lesser houses.
staying an ear distance away.

One night in a freak storm,
Lightning struck mary,
and threw her off the car,
and onto the roadside.

As she lay,
Windows broken,
and Attic spilled out onto the pavement
We both had to admit,
that taking a house out on the road,
was a pretty dangerous thing.

Mary lives back home now
And has had a makeover after
the accident.
With a brand new and sparse attic,
I have a spare key.

www.ingramcontent.com/pod-product-compliance
Lightning Source LLC
Chambersburg PA
CBHW041520220426
43667CB00002B/48